TOSEL®
STARTER

International TOSEL Committee

GRAMMAR 1

CONTENTS

Starter

TOSEL® Level Chart   TOSEL 단계표

COCOON

아이들이 접할 수 있는 공식 인증 시험의 첫 단계로써, 아이들의 부담을 줄이고 즐겁게 흥미를 유발할 수 있도록 컬러풀한 색상과 디자인으로 시험지를 구성하였습니다.

Pre-STARTER

친숙한 주제에 대한 단어, 짧은 대화, 짧은 문장을 사용한 기본적인 문장표현 능력을 측정합니다.

STARTER

흔히 접할 수 있는 주제와 상황과 관련된 주제에 대한 짧은 대화 및 짧은 문장을 이해하고 일상생활 대화에 참여하며 실질적인 영어 기초 의사소통 능력을 측정합니다.

BASIC

개인 정보와 일상 활동, 미래 계획, 과거의 경험에 대해 구어와 문어의 형태로 의사소통을 할 수 있는 능력을 측정합니다.

JUNIOR

일반적인 주제와 상황을 다루는 회화와 짧은 단락, 실용문, 짧은 연설 등을 이해하고 간단한 일상 대화에 참여하는 능력을 측정합니다.

HIGH JUNIOR

넓은 범위의 사회적, 학문적 주제에서 영어를 유창하고 정확하게, 효과적으로 사용할 수 있는 능력 및 중문과 복잡한 문장을 포함한 다양한 문장구조의 사용 능력을 측정합니다.

ADVANCED

대학 및 대학원에서 요구되는 영어능력과 취업 또는 직업근무환경에 필요한 실용영어 능력을 측정합니다.

COCOON
유치원생
영어의 첫 걸음 단계

Pre-STARTER
초등 1,2학년
영어를 시작하는 단계

STARTER
초등 3,4학년
영어의 밑바탕을 다지는 단계

BASIC
초등 5,6학년
영어의 도약 단계

JUNIOR
중학생
영어의 실전 단계

HIGH JUNIOR
고등학생
영어의 고급화 단계

ADVANCED
대학생,직장인
영어의 완성 단계

TOSEL
교재 Series

TOSEL LEVEL	Age	Vocabulary Frequency	Readability Score	교과 과정 연계	Grammar	VOCA	Reading	Listening
Cocoon	K5-K7	500	0-1	Who is he? (국어 1단원 1-1)	There is · There are	150	Picking Pumpkins (Phonics Story)	Phonics
Pre-Starter	P1-P2	700	1-2	How old are you? (통합교과 1-1)	be + adjective	300	Me & My Family (Reading series Ch.1)	묘사하기
Starter	P3-P4	1000-2000	1-2	Spring, Summer, Fall, Winter (통합교과 3-1)	Simple Present	800	Ask More Questions (Reading Series Ch.1)	날씨/시간 표현
Basic	P5-P6	3000-4000	3-4	Show and Tell (사회 5-1)	Superlative	1700	Culture (Reading Series Ch.3)	상대방 의견 묻고 답하기
Junior	M1-M2	5000-6000	5-6	중 1, 2 과학, 기술가정	to-infinitive	4000	Humans and Animals (Reading Series Ch.1)	정보 묻고 답하기
High Junior	H1-H3	5000-6000	5-6	고등학교 - 체육	2nd Conditional	7000	Health (Reading Series Ch.1)	사건 묘사하기

■ TOSEL의 세분화된 레벨은 각 연령에 맞는 어휘와 읽기 지능 및 교과 과정과의 연계가 가능하도록 설계된 교재들로 효과적인 학습 커리큘럼을 제공합니다.

■ TOSEL의 커리큘럼에 따른 학습은

정확한 레벨링 → 레벨에 적합한 학습 → 영어 능력 인증 시험 TOSEL에서의 공신력 있는 평가를 통해

진단 → 학습 → 평가의 선순환 구조를 실현합니다.

About TOSEL®

TOSEL은 각급 학교 교과과정과 연령별 인지단계를 고려하여 단계별 난이도와 문항으로
영어 숙달 정도를 측정하는 영어 사용자 중심의 맞춤식 영어능력인증 시험제도입니다.
평가유형에 따른 개인별 장점과 단점을 파악하고, 개인별 영어학습 방향을 제시하는 성적분석자료를 제공하여
영어능력 종합검진 서비스를 제공함으로써 영어 사용자인 소비자와
영어능력 평가를 토대로 영어교육을 담당하는 교사 및 기관 인사관리자인 공급자를
모두 만족시키는 영어능력인증 평가입니다.

TOSEL은 인지적-학문적 언어 사용의 유창성 (Cognitive-Academic Language Proficiency, CALP)과
기본적-개인적 의사소통능력 (Basic Interpersonal Communication Skill, BICS)을
엄밀히 구분하여 수험자의 언어능력을 가장 친밀하게 평가하는 시험입니다.

대상	목적	용도
유아, 초, 중, 고등학생, 대학생 및 직장인 등 성인	한국인의 영어구사능력 증진과 비영어권 국가의 영어 사용자의 영어구사능력 증진	실질적인 영어구사능력 평가 + 입학전형 및 인재선발 등에 활용 및 직무역량별 인재 배치

연혁

2002.02	국제토셀위원회 창설 (수능출제위원역임 전국대학 영어전공교수진 중심)
2004.09	TOSEL 고려대학교 국제어학원 공동인증시험 실시
2006.04	EBS 한국교육방송공사 주관기관 참여
2006.05	민족사관고등학교 입학전형에 반영
2008.12	고려대학교 편입학시험 TOSEL 유형으로 대체
2009.01	서울시 공무원 근무평정에 TOSEL 점수 가산점 부여
2009.01	전국 대부분 외고, 자사고 입학전형에 TOSEL 반영
	(한영외국어고등학교, 한일고등학교, 고양외국어고등학교, 과천외국어고등학교, 김포외국어고등학교, 명지외국어고등학교, 부산국제외국어고등학교, 부일외국어 고등학교, 성남외국어고등학교, 인천외국어고등학교, 전북외국어고등학교, 대전외국어고등학교, 청주외국어고등학교, 강원외국어고등학교, 전남외국어고등학교)
2009.12	청심국제중・고등학교 입학전형 TOSEL 반영
2009.12	한국외국어교육학회, 팬코리아영어교육학회, 한국음성학회, 한국응용언어학회 TOSEL 인증
2010.03	고려대학교, TOSEL 출제기관 및 공동 인증기관으로 참여
2010.07	경찰청 공무원 임용 TOSEL 성적 가산점 부여
2014.04	전국 200개 초등학교 단체 응시 실시
2017.03	중앙일보 주관기관 참여
2018.11	관공서, 대기업 등 100여 개 기관에서 TOSEL 반영
2019.06	미얀마 TOSEL 도입 발족식
	베트남 TOSEL 도입 협약식
2019.11	고려대학교 편입학전형 반영
2020.06	국토교통부 국가자격시험 TOSEL 반영
2021.07	소방청 간부후보생 선발시험 TOSEL 반영
2021.11	고려대학교 공과대학 기계학습・빅데이터 연구원 AI 연구 협약
2022.05	AI 영어학습 플랫폼 TOSEL Lab 공개
2023.11	고려대학교 경영대학 전국 고등학생 대상 정기캠퍼스 투어 프로그램 후원기관 참여
2024.01	제1회 TOSEL VOCA 올림피아드 실시
2024.03	고려대학교 미래교육원 TOSEL 전문가과정 개설

About TOSEL®

What's TOSEL?

"Test of Skills in the English Language"

TOSEL은 비영어권 국가의 영어 사용자를 대상으로 영어구사능력을 측정하여
그 결과를 공식 인증하는 영어능력인증 시험제도입니다.

영어 사용자 중심의 맞춤식 영어능력 인증 시험제도

맞춤식 평가

**획일적인 평가에서
세분화된 평가로의 전환**

TOSEL은 응시자의 연령별 인지단계에
따라 별도의 문항과 난이도를 적용하여
평가함으로써 평가의 목적과 용도에
적합한 평가 시스템을
구축하였습니다.

공정성과 신뢰성 확보

국제토셀위원회의 역할

TOSEL은 고려대학교가 출제 및 인증기관
으로 참여하였고 대학입학수학능력시험
출제위원 교수들이 중심이 된
국제토셀위원회가 주관하여
사회적 공정성과 신뢰성을 확보한
평가 제도입니다.

수입대체 효과

외화유출 차단 및 국위선양

TOSEL은 해외시험응시로 인한 외화의
유출을 막는 수입대체의 효과를 기대할
수 있습니다. TOSEL의 문항과 시험제도는
비영어권 국가에 수출하여 국위선양에
기여하고 있습니다.

Why TOSEL®

왜 TOSEL인가

01 학교 시험 폐지

일선 학교에서 중간, 기말고사 폐지로 인해 객관적인 영어 평가 제도의 부재가 우려됩니다. 그러나 전국단위로 연간 4번 시행되는 TOSEL 평가시험을 통해 학생들은 정확한 역량과 체계적인 학습방향을 꾸준히 진단받을 수 있습니다.

02 연령별/단계별 대비로 영어학습 점검

TOSEL은 응시자의 연령별 인지단계 및 영어 학습 단계에 따라 총 7단계로 구성되었습니다. 각 단계에 알맞은 문항유형과 난이도를 적용해 모든 연령 및 학습 과정에 맞추어 가장 효율적으로 영어실력을 평가할 수 있도록 개발된 영어시험입니다.

03 학교내신성적 향상

TOSEL은 학년별 교과과정과 연계하여 학교에서 배우는 내용을 학습하고 평가할 수 있도록 문항 및 주제를 구성하여 내신영어 향상을 위한 최적의 솔루션을 제공합니다.

04 수능대비 직결

유아, 초, 중등시절 어렵지 않고 즐겁게 학습해 온 영어이지만, 수능시험준비를 위해 접하는 영어의 문항 및 유형 난이도에 주춤하게 됩니다. 이를 대비하기 위해 TOSEL은 유아부터 성인까지 점진적인 학습을 통해 수능대비를 자연적으로 해나갈 수 있습니다.

05 진학과 취업에 대비한 필수 스펙관리

개인별 '학업성취기록부' 발급을 통해 영어학업성취이력을 꾸준히 기록한 영어학습 포트폴리오를 제공하여 영어학습 이력을 관리할 수 있습니다.

06 자기소개서에 토셀 기재

개별적인 진로 적성 Report를 제공하여 진로를 파악하고 자기소개서 작성시 적극적으로 활용할 수 있는 객관적인 자료를 제공합니다.

07 영어학습 동기부여

시험실시 후 응시자 모두에게 수여되는 인증서는 영어학습에 대한 자신감과 성취감을 고취시키고 동기를 부여합니다.

08 AI 분석 영어학습 솔루션

국내외 15,000여 개 학교·학원 단체 응시인원 중 엄선한 100만 명 이상의 실제 TOSEL 성적 데이터를 기반으로 영어인증시험 제도 중 세계 최초로 인공지능이 분석한 개인별 AI 정밀 진단 성적표를 제공합니다. 최첨단 AI 정밀진단 성적표는 최적의 영어 학습 솔루션을 제시하여 영어 학습에 소요되는 시간과 노력을 획기적으로 절감해줍니다.

09 명예의 전당, 우수협력기관 지정

우수교육기관은 'TOSEL 우수 협력 기관'에 지정되고, 각 시/도별, 최고득점자를 명예의 전당에 등재합니다.

Evaluation ——— 평가

평가의 기본원칙
TOSEL은 PBT(Paper Based Test)를 통하여 간접평가와 직접평가를 모두 시행합니다.

TOSEL은 언어의 네 가지 요소인 **읽기, 듣기, 말하기, 쓰기 영역을 모두 평가합니다.**

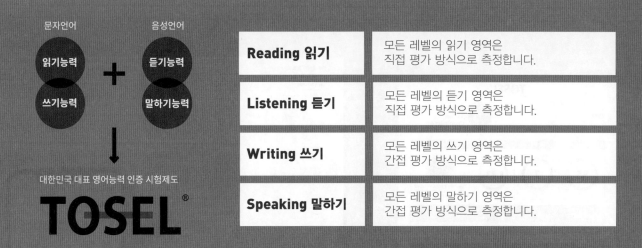

Reading 읽기	모든 레벨의 읽기 영역은 직접 평가 방식으로 측정합니다.
Listening 듣기	모든 레벨의 듣기 영역은 직접 평가 방식으로 측정합니다.
Writing 쓰기	모든 레벨의 쓰기 영역은 간접 평가 방식으로 측정합니다.
Speaking 말하기	모든 레벨의 말하기 영역은 간접 평가 방식으로 측정합니다.

문자언어 · 음성언어
읽기능력 + 듣기능력
쓰기능력 · 말하기능력

대한민국 대표 영어능력 인증 시험제도
TOSEL®

TOSEL은 연령별 인지단계를 고려하여 **아래와 같이 7단계로 나누어 평가합니다.**

1 단계	**TOSEL®** COCOON	**5~7세의 미취학 아동**
2 단계	**TOSEL®** Pre-STARTER	**초등학교 1~2학년**
3 단계	**TOSEL®** STARTER	**초등학교 3~4학년**
4 단계	**TOSEL®** BASIC	**초등학교 5~6학년**
5 단계	**TOSEL®** JUNIOR	**중학생**
6 단계	**TOSEL®** HIGH JUNIOR	**고등학생**
7 단계	**TOSEL®** ADVANCED	**대학생 및 성인**

Grade Report ————— 성적표 및 인증서

고도화 성적표: 응시자 개인별 최적화 AI 정밀진단

20여년간 축적된 약 100만명 이상의 엄선된 응시자 빅데이터를 TOSEL AI로 분석·진단한 개인별 성적자료

전국 단위 연령, 레벨 통계자료를 활용하여 보다 정밀한 성취 수준 판별
파트별 강/약점, 영역별 역량, 8가지 지능, 단어 수준 등을 비교 및 분석하여 폭넓은 학습 진단
오답 문항 유형별 심층 분석 자료 및 솔루션으로 학습 방향 제시, TOSEL과 수능 및 교과학습 성취기준과의 연계
모바일 기기 지원 - UX/UI 개선, 반응형 웹페이지로 구현되어 태블릿, 휴대폰, PC 등 다양한 기기 환경에서 접근 가능

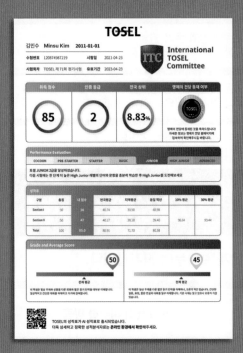

기본 제공 성적표

고도화 성적표 (일부 유료)

단체 성적 분석 자료

단체 및 기관 대상

- 레벨별 평균성적추이, 학생분포
  섹션 및 영역별 평균 점수, 표준편차

TOSEL Lab 지정교육기관 대상 추가 제공

- 원생 별 취약영역 분석 및 보강방안 제시
- TOSEL수험심리척도를 바탕으로 학생의 응답 특이성을
  파악하여 코칭 방안 제시
- 전국 및 지역 단위 종합적 비교분석
  (레벨/유형별 응시자 연령 및 규모, 최고득점 등)

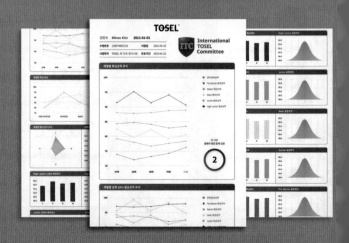

'토셀 명예의 전당' 등재

특별시, 광역시, 도 별 **1등 선발**
(7개시 9개도 **1등 선발**)

*홈페이지 로그인 – 시험결과 – 명예의 전당에서
  해당자 등재 증명서 출력 가능

'학업성취기록부'에 토셀 인증등급 기재

개인별 **'학업성취기록부'** 평생 발급
진학과 취업을 대비한 **필수 스펙관리**

인증서

대한민국 초,중,고등학생의 영어숙달능력 평가 결과 공식인증

고려대학교 인증획득 (2010. 03)

한국외국어교육학회 인증획득 (2009. 12)

한국음성학회 인증획득 (2009. 12)

한국응용언어학회 인증획득 (2009. 11)

팬코리아영어교육학회 인증획득 (2009. 10)

Grammar Series ——— 특장점

TOSEL 시험을 기준으로 빈출 지표를 활용한 문법 선정 및 예문과 문제 구성

TOSEL 시험 활용

- ■ 실제 TOSEL 시험에 출제된 빈출 문항을 기준으로 단계별 학습을 위한 문법 선정

- ■ 실제 TOSEL 시험에 활용된 문장을 사용하여 예문과 문제를 구성

- ■ 문법 학습 이외에 TOSEL 기출 문제 풀이를 통해서 TOSEL 및 실전 영어 시험 대비 학습

세분화된 레벨링

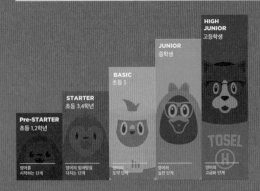

20년 간 대한민국 영어 평가 기관으로서

연간 4회 전국적으로 실시되는 정기시험에서

축적된 성적 데이터를 기반으로

정확하고 세분화된 레벨링을 통한

영어 학습 콘텐츠 개발

언어의 4대 영역 균형 학습 + 평가

1. TOSEL 평가: 학생의 영어 능력을 정확하게 평가

2. 결과 분석 및 진단: 시험 점수와 결과를 분석하여 학생의 강점, 취약점, 학습자 특성 등을 객관적으로 진단

3. 학습 방향 제시: 객관적 진단 데이터를 기반으로 학습자 특성에 맞는 학습 방향 제시 및 목표 설정

4. 학습: 제시된 방향과 목표에 따라 학생에게 적합한 문법 학습법 소개 및 영어의 체계와 구조 이해

5. 학습 목표 달성: 학습 후 다시 평가를 통해 목표 달성 여부 확인 및 성장을 위한 다음 학습 목표 설정

Grammar Series ——— Level

TOSEL의 Grammar Series는 레벨에 맞게 단계적으로
문법을 학습할 수 있도록 구성되어 있습니다.

Pre-Starter	Starter	Basic	Junior	High Junior

- ■ 그림을 활용하여 문법에 대한 이해도 향상
- ■ 다양한 활동을 통해 문법 반복 학습 유도
- ■ TOSEL 기출 문제 연습을 통한 실전 대비

- ■ TOSEL 기출의 빈도수를 활용한 문법 선정으로 효율적 학습
- ■ 실제 TOSEL 지문의 예문을 활용한 실용적 학습 제공
- ■ TOSEL 기출 문제 연습을 통한 실전 대비

최신 수능 출제
문법을 포함하여
수능 대비 가능

1시간 학습 Guideline

01 💡 Unit Intro

5분

- 초등 교육과정에서 익혀야 하는 문법과 단어를 중심으로 단원의 표현에 대해 미리 생각해보기

02 📖 개념

10분

- Unit Intro의 회화 표현을 따라 읽으며, 관련 문법에 대한 학습

05 ✏️ Practice

10분

- Unit에서 배운 문법을 활용하여 문제 해결하기
- 틀린 문제에 대해서는 해당 Unit에서 복습하도록 지도하기

06 📖 Writing Activity

5분

- 빈도수가 높은 주요 단어 위주로 writing activity를 추가하여 쓰기 학습 지도
- 단어를 소리 내어 읽으며, 점선을 따라 스펠링을 쓰도록 지도하기

03  Activity

3분

- 배운 문법을 활용하여 문제 해결하기
- 빈칸 채우기, 알맞은 표현 고르기 등 TOSEL 실전 문제 학습
- 함께 문제를 풀며 학생들이 즐겁게 단어를 학습할 수 있도록 유도하기

04 Exercise

10분

- 다양한 Exercise 활동을 하며 혼동하기 쉬운 문법 학습

07 Unit Review

2분

- 빈 칸을 채우는 형태로 구성하여 수업 시간 후 복습에 용이하게 구성
- 배운 문법을 직접 활용하여 수업 시간 후 복습에 용이하게 구성

08 TOSEL 실전문제

15분

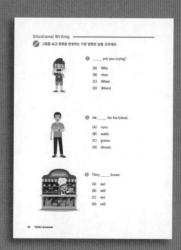

- 실제 TOSEL 기출 문제를 통한 실전 대비 학습
- 실제 시험 시간과 유사하게 풀이할 수 있도록 지도하기
- 틀린 문제에 대해서는 해당 단원에서 복습하도록 지도하기

PreStarter/Starter/Basic Syllabus

PreStarter		Basic		2015 개정 초등 영어 언어형식
Chapter	Unit	Chapter	Unit	
I. 명사: 명사는 이름이야	1 셀 수 있는 명사	I. 명사	1 셀 수 있는 명사 앞에 붙는 관사 the/a/an	A boy/The **boy**/The (two) boys ran in the park. **The** store is closed.
	2 셀 수 있는 명사 앞에 붙는 관사 a/an		2 셀 수 없는 명사를 측정하는 단위	**Water** is very important for life. **Kate** is from **London**.
	3 셀 수 없는 명사		3 규칙 복수명사	The **two boys** ran in the park.
	4 명사의 복수형		4 불규칙 복수명사	
II. 대명사: 명사를 대신하는 대명사	1 주격 대명사	II. 대명사	1 단수대명사의 격	**She** is a teacher, and **he**'s a scientist. I like **your** glasses. What about **mine**?
	2 소유격 대명사		2 복수대명사의 격	**They**'re really delicious. **We** are very glad to hear from him.
	3 목적격 대명사		3 1, 2인칭 대명사의 활용	I like math, but Susan doesn't like **it**. He will help **you**.
	4 지시대명사		4 3인칭 대명사의 활용	Which do you like better, **this** or **that**? **These** are apples, and **those** are tomatoes. **That** dog is smart. **These/Those** books are really large.
III. 형용사: 명사&대명사를 꾸미는 형용사	1 형용사의 명사수식	III. 동사	1 동사의 기본시제	He **walks** to school every day. We **played** soccer yesterday. She **is going to** visit her grandparents next week. He **is sleeping** now. I **will visit** America next year.
	2 형용사의 대명사수식		2 동사의 불규칙 과거형	
	3 숫자와 시간		3 헷갈리기 쉬운 동사	**It's half past four.** **What time** is it?
				I **don't** like snakes. We **didn't** enjoy the movie very much.
	4 지시형용사		4 조동사	She **can** play the violin. Tom **won't** be at the meeting tomorrow. I **will** visit America next year. You **may** leave now.

Junior Syllabus

Junior		2015 개정 중등 영어 언어형식
Chapter	Unit	
I. 8품사 (1)	1 명사	She lived in the **woods** when she was kid. Thank you for your **kindness**.
	2 대명사	I have **three books**. **One** is mine. **The others** are yours. **The chocolate cookie** is sweet. I'm going to have **another one**.
	3 형용사	Something **strange** happened last night.
	4 감탄사	**How** beautiful she is! **What** a player!
II 8품사 (2)	1 동사	**Mathematics** is my favorite subject. **Each** boy admires his teacher. **Both** the teacher **and** the students enjoyed the class. You can have **either** tea or coffee. It is **not only** beautiful **but (also)** useful.
	2 부사	
	3 전치사	
	4 접속사	I may stop by tomorrow **or** just phone you. **Both** the teacher **and** the students enjoyed the class.
III. 문장의 구조	1 문장성분의 기초	You can **put the dish on the table**. He **gave me a present**. They **elected him president**.
	2 문장의 형식	
	3 평서문의 전환	
	4 의문문의 비교	**Have you** finished your homework yet? This is your book, **isn't it**?
IV. 문장의 시제	1 단순시제	I **will be** able to help you get to the party tonight. **Are you going** to take the last train?
	2 진행시제	**I'm thinking** about the problem. I **was studying** when John called me.
	3 현재완료	The bakery **has been** open since 1960. He **has attended** the club meetings regularly.
	4 시간을 나타내는 접속사	**Since** he left this morning, I haven't seen him. **When** we arrived, she was talking on the phone.
V. to부정사와 동명사	1 to부정사	**To see** is **to belive**. Chris was glad **to hear the news**.
	2 동명사	We **enjoy swimming** in the pool. Life is **worth living**. I'm interested in **watching horror movies**.
	3 to부정사와 동명사 비교	
	4 의미상주어	It is difficult **for me to speak French**. It was kind **of you to help us**.
VI. 비교급과 최상급	1 비교급과 최상급의 규칙 변화	They've got **more/less** money **than** they need. A car is **much more** expensive **than** a motorbike.
	2 비교급과 최상급의 불규칙 변화	
	3 원급의 비교	You can run **as fast as** Billy can. She is old, but she is not **as old as** he (is).
	4 최상급의 비교	Cindy is **the shortest** of the three. It is **the most interesting** speech I've ever heard.

High Junior Syllabus

High Junior		2015 개정 중등 영어 언어형식
Chapter	**Unit**	
I. 문장의 형성	1 8품사와 문장 성분	The audience is/are enjoying the show. I'd like to **write a diary**, but I'm too busy to do so. He's being very rude. We **are hoping** you will be with us.
	2 문장의 형식	
	3 문장의 배열	I think (that) he is a good actor. Although/Though it was cold, I went swimming.
	4 문장의 강조	The weather was **so** nice **that** we went hiking. It was Justin who/that told me the truth.
II 부정사와 동명사	1 원형부정사	You shouldn't **let him go** there again. I **heard** the children **sing/singing**.
	2 to부정사	He seemed **to have been ill (for some time)**. Bill promised Jane **to work out with her**. I remembered **John/John's coming late for class**. It goes without **saying that time is money**. There is no use **crying over the spilt milk**.
	3 동명사	
	4 to부정사와 동명사구	
III. 분사	1 현재분사	At the station I met a lady **carrying a large umbrella**. **With the night coming**, stars began to shine in the sky.
	2 과거분사	Wallets **found on the street** must be reported to the police.
	3 분사구문	**Walking along the street**, I met an old friend. **Having seen that movie before**, I wanted to see it again.
	4 독립분사구문	**Joshua returning home**, the puppy ran toward him. **Frankly speaking**, I failed the test.
IV. 수동태	1 수동태의 형성	The building **was built** in 1880. I **was made** to clean the room. Nolan **was seen** to enter the building. The monkey **has been raised** by human parents for years. Cooper **will be invited** to today's meeting. The information superhighway **will have been introduced** to everyone by 2015.
	2 수동태와 능동태의 전환	
	3 수동태와 전치사의 사용	
	4 주의해야 할 수동태 용법	
V. 관계대명사와 관계부사	1 관계대명사의 사용	The girl **who is playing the piano** is called Ann. This is the book (that) I bought yesterday.
	2 관계대명사와 선행사	Please tell me **what happened**.
	3 관계대명사의 생략	This is **why** we have to study English grammar.
	4 관계부사	The town **in which I was born** is very small. That's just **how he talks**, always serious about his work.
VI. 가정법	1 가정법 현재와 과거	**If it were not for you, I would** be lonely.
	2 가정법 과거완료	**Had** I had enough money, I **would have bought** a cell phone. **Without/But for** your advice, I **would have** failed.
	3 혼합가정법	I **wish** I **had learned** swimming last summer. He acts **as if** he **had been** there.
	4 특수가정법	I'd **rather** we **had** dinner now. **Provided that/As long as** they had plenty to eat, the crew **seemed** to be happy.

CHAPTER 01

Unit 01

What do you do?

네 직업이 무엇이니?

I ⬚⬚⬚⬚⬚ a firefighter.

문장과 함께 개념을 학습해보세요.

Q: What do you do?　　　　　　　　네 직업이 무엇이니?
A: I _____ a teacher.　　　　　　나 ____ 선생님이야.

be동사는 '~이다'라는 뜻이야.
am, are, is 세 개를 be동사라고 불러.

be동사가 쓰이는 곳은 정말 많아. 예를 들어서 직업을 소개하거나,

I am a student.　　　　She is a vet.　　　　He is a pianist.

특징을 표현할 때에도 쓸 수 있지.

You are smart.　　　　They are kind.　　　　We are busy.

I	am
he, she, it	is
you, they, we	are

Activity

알맞은 명사와 연결해보세요.

1 he ●

2 you ●

● am

3 they ●

● are

4 I ●

● is

5 it ●

6 she ●

Exercise

그림을 보고 빈칸에 알맞은 be동사를 넣어 문장을 완성하세요.

1 He ⬚⬚⬚ a firefighter.

2 You ⬚⬚⬚ busy.

3 She ⬚⬚⬚ smart.

4 I _____ a pianist.

5 He _____ kind.

6 She _____ angry.

Practice

그림을 보고 알맞은 문장을 고르세요.

1. (A) They is vets.
   (B) They am vets.
   (C) They are vets.

2. (A) It is for baseball.
   (B) It are for baseball.
   (C) It am for baseball.

3. (A) She is sick.
   (B) She am sick.
   (C) She are sick.

4 (A) It is a pear.
(B) It are a pear.
(C) It am a pear.

5 (A) He is in the bank.
(B) He am in the bank.
(C) He are in the bank.

6 (A) I is angry.
(B) I am angry.
(C) I are angry.

 **Writing Activity**

1 student
학생

student

2 vet
수의사

vet

3 pianist
피아니스트

pianist

4 smart
똑똑한

smart

5 kind
착한

kind

6 busy
바쁜

7 balloon
풍선

8 bank
은행

9 pear
배

10 ball
공

Unit Review

다음 대화를 완성하고, 소리내어 연습해보세요.

Jimmy

What do you do?

I am a pianist.

What do you do?

Ken

Jimmy

I am a firefighter.

Unit 02

What are you going to do during the vacation?

너는 방학 동안 무엇을 할 계획이니?

I'm going to _____.

문장과 함께 개념을 학습해보세요.

Q: **What are you going to do during the vacation?**
너는 방학동안 무엇을 할 계획이니?
A: **I'm going to**   **.**
나는   에 가.

질문을 할 때 쓰는 말들을 의문사라고 해.
'누가, 언제, 어디서, 무엇을, 어떻게, 왜' 육하원칙을 기억하자.

who	누가	what	무엇을
when	언제	how	어떻게
where	어디서	why	왜

who

Q: **Who is he?**

A: **He is my uncle.**

when

Q: **When do you sleep?**

A: **At 9 o'clock.**

where

Q: **Where are you going?**

A: **I'm going to the church.**

what

Q: **What are you doing?**

A: **I'm watching a movie.**

how

Q: **How** is she?

A: **She is okay now.**

why

Q: **Why** are they crying?

A: **I don't know.**

Activity

알맞은 명사와 연결해보세요.

1. what   ●

2. where   ●

3. why   ●

4. how   ●

5. who   ●

6. when   ●

● 어디서

● 왜

● 언제

● 누가

● 어떻게

● 무엇을

Exercise

그림을 보고 빈칸에 알맞은 의문사를 넣어 문장을 완성하세요.

1 _____ **is our vacation?**

2 _____ **is the church?**

3 _____ **are you thinking?**

4   **is she crying?**

5   **is your uncle?**

6   **is he?**

Practice

그림을 보고 알맞은 문장을 고르세요.

1
(A) Why is the bank?
(B) When is the bank?
(C) Where is the bank?

2
(A) Why are you?
(B) How are you?
(C) What are you?

3
(A) Who are you going to sleep?
(B) How are you going to sleep?
(C) When are you going to sleep?

4
(A) Who is your teacher?
(B) What is your teacher?
(C) When is your teacher?

5
(A) Why are they going to study?
(B) How are they going to study?
(C) When are they going to study?

6
(A) Why is the bakery?
(B) What is the bakery?
(C) Where is the bakery?

1　**go**
　　　가다

2　**think**
　　　생각하다

3　**sleep**
　　　자다

4　**watch**
　　　보다

5　**cry**
　　　울다

6 now
지금

now

7 okay
알겠다

okay

8 church
교회

church

9 bakery
빵집 · 제과점

bakery

10 uncle
삼촌

uncle

Unit Review

다음 대화를 완성하고, 소리내어 연습해보세요.

Alice

What are you going to do during the vacation?

I'm still thinking about what to do. How about you?

Mike

Alice

I want to go swimming.

Unit 03

What is her hobby?

그녀의 취미는 무엇이니?

She singing.

문장과 함께 개념을 학습해보세요.

Q: What is her hobby?   그녀의 취미는 무엇이니?
A: She _____ dancing.   그녀는 춤추는 것을 _____.

움직이는 게 바로 동사야.
행동이나 '~하다'라는 뜻을 가진 말들을 동사라고 해.

동사는 사람이 직접 하는 행동들을 나타낼 수도 있고,

give a present   **drink** water   **eat** pizza

마음을 표현할 수도 있고,

like   hate

상황을 묘사할 수도 있어.

grow

die

melt

Activity

알맞은 동사와 연결해보세요.

1 grow ●   ● 싫어하다

2 give ●   ● 먹다

3 like ●   ● 자라다

4 eat ●   ● 좋아하다

5 hate ●   ● 주다

Exercise

그림을 보고 빈칸에 알맞은 동사를 넣어 문장을 완성하세요.

1 He d⬜⬜⬜⬜⬜ water.

2 She s⬜⬜⬜⬜ a song.

3 He g⬜⬜⬜⬜ a book.

4 He e ⬜⬜⬜ chicken.

5 My older brother h ⬜⬜⬜⬜ studying.

6 A chick g ⬜⬜⬜⬜.

Practice

그림을 보고 알맞은 문장을 고르세요.

1
(A) She on the chair sits.
(B) She sits on the chair.
(C) She chair sits on the.

2
(A) He the window closes.
(B) Closes he the window.
(C) He closes the window.

3
(A) The birds fly in the air.
(B) The birds in the air fly.
(C) The birds air in the fly.

4
(A) He stands on the stage.
(B) He stage on the stands.
(C) He on the stands stage.

5
(A) She hands her claps.
(B) She claps her hands.
(C) She her claps hands.

6
(A) Melts ice the.
(B) The melts ice.
(C) The ice melts.

 **Writing Activity**

1 **hobby**
취미

2 **sing**
노래하다

3 **give**
주다

4 **present**
선물

5 **drink**
마시다

6   **eat**
먹다

7   **hate**
싫어하다

8   **grow**
자라다

9   **die**
죽다

10   **melt**
녹다

Unit Review

다음 대화를 완성하고, 소리내어 연습해보세요.

Sarah

What is your sister's hobby?

She likes singing.

How about yours?

Amy

Sarah

She likes dancing.

Unit 04

What are you doing?

너는 무엇을 하는 중이니?

I am _____.

문장과 함께 개념을 학습해보세요.

Q: **What are you doing?** 너는 무엇을 하는 중이니?
A: **I am** _____ . 나는 _____ .

영어도 한국어처럼 시간을 표현해.
'과거-현재-미래' 중에서 지금을 나타내는 게 현재야.

우리가 지금까지 배운 것들은 대부분 현재시제 동사야.
동사의 원래 모습 그대로가 현재시제로 쓰여.

write

dance

jump

use

run

play

한국어와 달리, 영어에서의 시간은 복잡해.
'과거-현재-미래' 외에, 진행시제랑 완료시제라는 게 있어.

현재진행시제는 지금 당장 하고 있는 일에 -ing를 붙이기만 하면 돼.
-e로 끝나는 말은 -e를 빼고 -ing를 붙여.

walk → **walking**

study → **studying**

ride → **riding**

Activity

올바른 현재진행시제 문장의 번호를 쓰세요.

① We are riding.

② She studied.

③ She is jumping.

④ I jump.

⑤ They are walking.

⑥ He is dancing.

Exercise

다음 보기에서 단어를 골라, 알맞은 형태로 빈칸을 완성하세요.

보기   walk   ride   study   dance   write   swim

1 **She** _____ **a bike.**

2 **I** _____ **a letter.**

3 **They** _____ **in the lake.**

4 They are [____].

5 He is [____] with her.

6 We are [____] in the park.

Practice

그림을 보고 알맞은 문장을 고르세요.

1
(A) He jump into the water.
(B) He jumps into the water.
(C) He jumping into the water.

2
(A) I use a computer.
(B) I uses a computer.
(C) I using a computer.

3
(A) She runs.
(B) She is run.
(C) She running.

4

(A) He finish his homework.

(B) He finishes his homework.

(C) He finishing his homework.

5

(A) She is wash her hands.

(B) She washes her hands.

(C) She is washes her hands.

6

(A) They find him.

(B) They are find him.

(C) They are finds him.

1 swim
수영하다

2 dance
춤추다

3 use
사용하다

4 play
놀다

5 study
공부하다

6 write
쓰다

7 jump
뛰다

8 run
달리다

9 walk
걷다

10 ride
타다

Unit Review

다음 대화를 완성하고, 소리내어 연습해보세요.

Wendy

What are you doing?

I am studying.

What are you doing?

Alice

Wendy

I am playing baseball.

TOSEL 실전문제 ❶

Situational Writing

 그림을 보고 문장을 완성하는 가장 알맞은 답을 고르세요.

1 _____ are you crying?

(A)   Why

(B)   How

(C)   When

(D)   Where

2 He _____ for his friend.

(A)   runs

(B)   waits

(C)   grows

(D)   shouts

3 They _____ bread.

(A)   eat

(B)   sell

(C)   eet

(D)   cell

4 _____ is the hospital?

(A)   How

(B)   What

(C)   When

(D)   Where

5 The children _____ baseball.

(A)   play

(B)   plaied

(C)   playing

(D)   are played

6 He _____ magic to his classmates.

(A)   shew

(B)   shows

(C)   showing

(D)   are shown

Sentence Completion

 빈칸에 들어갈 가장 알맞은 답을 고르세요.

1 She _____ her hands.

(A) wash

(B) washs

(C) washes

(D) washing

2 He _____ tall.

(A) is

(B) am

(C) are

(D) can

3 The bird _____ high.

(A) fly

(B) flys

(C) flies

(D) flying

4 They _____ forward the finish li▮

(A) run

(B) runs

(C) runns

(D) runner

5 _____ is your daughter?

(A) Who

(B) Why

(C) How

(D) What

6 She _____ a queen.

(A) is
(B) am
(C) are
(D) can

9 _____ is your vacation?

(A) Who
(B) What
(C) When
(D) Where

7 They _____ busy.

(A) is
(B) am
(C) are
(D) being

10 Grace _____ math.

(A) study
(B) studys
(C) studies
(D) studying

8 This book _____ hard.

(A) is
(B) am
(C) are
(D) being

CHAPTER 02

Unit 01

How does she walk?

그녀는 어떻게 걷니?

She walks ███████████████████ **.**

문장과 함께 개념을 학습해보세요.

Q: How does she walk?   그녀는 어떻게 걷니?
A: She walks _____ .   그녀는 _____ 걸어.

주로 **동사를 꾸며주는**게 **부사야.**
-ly로 끝나는 말들이 대부분 부사라고 생각하면 돼.

부사는 동사만 있을 때보다 더 풍부한 뜻을 전할 수 있게 해줘.

run slow**ly**

move quick**ly**

think bad**ly**

sing loud**ly**

speak quiet**ly**

cry sad**ly**

부사는 동사만 있을 때보다 더 풍부한 뜻을 전할 수 있게 해줘.

swim easi**ly**

dance happi**ly**

Activity

공부한 부사들로 빙고판을 완성하고 빙고 게임을 해보세요.

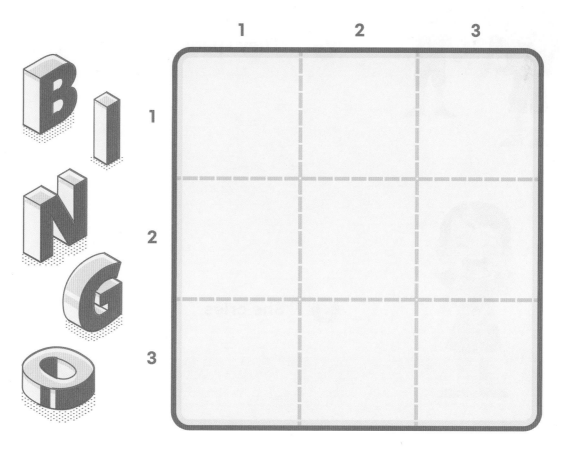

Exercise

다음 보기에서 단어를 골라, 알맞은 형태로 빈칸을 완성하세요.

보기   sad   slow   quiet   easy   loud   quick

1 **He runs** _____ **.**

2 **They speak** _____ **.**

3 **She cries** _____ **.**

4 I can make it ____.

5 We stay ____.

6 You run ____.

Practice

그림을 보고 알맞은 문장을 고르세요.

1
(A) We sing a song happy.
(B) We sing a song happily.
(C) We sing a song happyly.

2
(A) He acts bad.
(B) He acts baily.
(C) He acts badly.

3
(A) She moves quick.
(B) She moves quicily.
(C) She moves quickly.

4 (A) He picks a book careful.

(B) He picks a book carefully.

(C) He picks a book carefulily.

5 (A) The teacher treats us kind.

(B) The teacher treats us kindly.

(C) The teacher treats us kindily.

6 (A) He paints nice.

(B) He paints nicely.

(C) He paints niceily.

1 **slowly**
느리게

2 **quickly**
빠르게

3 **loudly**
크게

4 **quietly**
조용하게

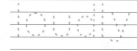

5 **easily**
쉽게

6 move
움직이다

move

7 badly
나쁘게

badly

8 speak
말하다

speak

9 sadly
슬프게

sadly

10 happily
행복하게

happily

Unit Review

다음 대화를 완성하고, 소리내어 연습해보세요.

Lily

How does she run?

She runs slowly.

Adrian

Lily

How about her brother?

He also runs slowly.

Adrian

Unit 02

Where are the cows?

소들은 어디에 있니?

They are standing ⬚⬚⬚⬚⬚⬚**.**

문장과 함께 개념을 학습해보세요.

Q: Where are the cows?
소들은 어디에 있니?

A: They are standing   .
그들은   서 있어.

-ly로 끝나는 말이 아닌 부사도 있어.
이런 부사도 똑같이 주로 동사를 꾸며주는 역할을 해.

부사는 동사를 꾸미기도 하고,

run **fast**

study **hard**

grow **well**

같은 부사를 꾸미기도 하고,

very much

so much

very well

형용사나 문장을 꾸미기도 하지.

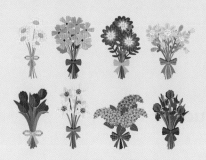

very pretty

Today I will go to school.

Activity

알맞은 부사와 연결해보세요.

① well ● ● 오늘

② hard ● ● 매우

③ very ● ● 잘

④ very much ● ● 열심히

⑤ fast ● ● 빠르게

⑥ today ● ● 아주

Exercise

그림을 보고 문장 안에 들어갈 부사를 완성하세요.

1 He studies h▢▢▢ .

2 She is v▢▢▢ pretty.

3 The rabbit runs f▢▢▢ .

4 The tree is s　big.

5 He eats too m　　　.

6 She has a birthday party
t　　　　.

Practice

그림을 보고 알맞은 문장을 고르세요.

1
(A) He dances very so.
(B) He dances very well.
(C) He dances very much.

2
(A) She works hard.
(B) She hard works.
(C) Hard she works.

3
(A) The man looks handsome very.
(B) The man very looks handsome.
(C) The man looks very handsome.

4 (A) We will today play soccer.
(B) We will play today soccer.
(C) We will play soccer today.

5 (A) Thank you very so.
(B) Thank you very well.
(C) Thank you very much.

6 (A) He swims so very.
(B) He swims very well.
(C) He swims very much.

 **Writing Activity**

1 **fast**
빠르게

2 **hard**
열심히

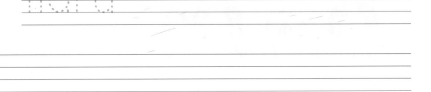

3 **well**
잘

4 **very**
아주

5 **much**
매우

6 so
정말로

7 pretty
예쁜

8 today
오늘

9 will
~할 것이다

10 school
학교

Unit Review

다음 대화를 완성하고, 소리내어 연습해보세요.

Sue

How does he run?

He runs fast.

Nick

Sue

How about his sister?
Does she also run fast?

Yes, she also runs fast.

Nick

Unit 03

Does he run fast?
그는 빠르게 달리니?

Yes, he is a _____ **runner.**

문장과 함께 개념을 학습해보세요.

Q: Does he run fast? 그는 빠르게 달리니?

A: Yes, he runs ⬚⬚⬚. 응, 그는 ⬚⬚ 달려.

형용사처럼 생긴 부사들이 있어.
둘은 똑같이 생겼지만 다르게 쓰여서 구분해야 해.

부사 - 형용사

run **fast** - **fast** runner

meet **early** - **early** meeting

live **long** - **long** life

think **right** - **right** thinking

Activity

색칠된 단어가 부사로 사용된 것에 동그라미 치세요.

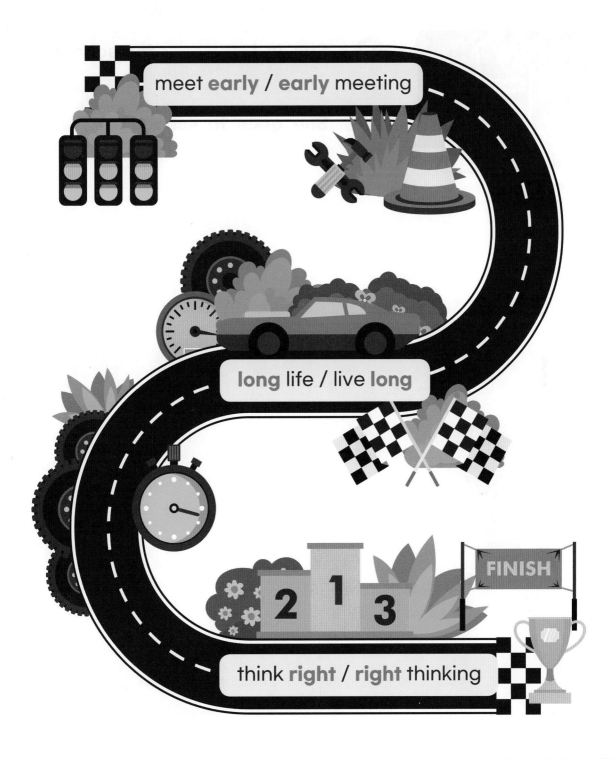

meet **early** / **early** meeting

long life / live **long**

think **right** / **right** thinking

Exercise

그림을 보고 문장 안에 들어갈 부사 또는 형용사를 완성하세요.

1 She is l ⬜⬜⬜ for school.

She goes to school l ⬜⬜⬜.

2 He is a f ⬜⬜⬜ runner.

He runs f ⬜⬜⬜.

3 We meet e ▢▢▢▢.

We have an e ▢▢▢▢ meeting.

4 They think r ▢▢▢▢.

They have r ▢▢▢▢▢ thinking.

Practice

그림을 보고 알맞은 문장을 고르세요.

1 (A) A monkey has a tail long.
(B) A monkey has a long tail.
(C) A monkey has long a tail.

2 (A) A horse fast run.
(B) A horse runs fast.
(C) A horse is animal fast.

3 (A) He writes right the answer.
(B) He right writes the answer.
(C) He writes the right answer.

4
(A) He lives hard a life.
(B) He lives a hard life.
(C) He hard lives a life.

5
(A) He tries to hard win.
(B) He hard tries to win.
(C) He tries hard to win.

6
(A) A monkey can high climb.
(B) A monkey can climb high.
(C) A monkey high can climb.

Writing Activity

1 **runner**
달리기 선수

runner

2 **meet**
만나다

meet

3 **early**
이른

early

4 **meeting**
회의

meeting

5 **live**
살다

live

6 **life**
삶

7 **right**
옳은

8 **thinking**
생각

9 **horse**
말

10 **glad**
기쁜

다음 대화를 완성하고, 소리내어 연습해보세요.

Gwen

Does she run fast?

Yes, she is a fast runner.
She goes jogging every morning.

Christina

Gwen

Does she get up early
in the morning?

Of course.

Christina

Unit 04

Are you hungry?

너 배고프니?

Yes, but I can't have lunch   .

문장과 함께 개념을 학습해보세요.

> Q: **Are you hungry?**
> 너 배고프니?
>
> A: **Yes, but I can't have lunch** _____ **.**
> 응, 그렇지만 나는 _____ 점심을 먹을 수 없어.

문장을 쓸 때에는 꼭 주어 다음에 동사를 써.
그런데 부사는 문장을 쓸 때 위치가 자유로운 편이야.

부사가 꾸며주려는 말 뒤에 오는 경우도 있고,

I can't have lunch **yet**.   I love you **too**.   He can run **fast**.

꾸며주려는 말 앞에 오는 경우도 있어.

Only my parents know me.   This is **just** for you.   I **still** love you.

그리고 꾸며주는 말 앞이나 뒤 상관없이 오는 경우도 있지!

Maybe we can go for a walk.
= We can go for a walk, **maybe**.

It is night **already**.
= It is **already** night.

Activity

올바른 문장을 고르세요.

1 Maybe she is sad. / She maybe is sad.

2 I had already lunch. / I already had lunch.

3 I love you too. / I love too you.

4 She still hates you. / She hates still you.

5 I yet didn't have lunch. / I didn't have lunch yet.

Exercise

그림을 보고 문장 안에 들어갈 부사를 완성하세요.

1 I love my sister t ☐ ☐ .

2 I haven't done my homework y ☐ ☐ .

3 I play computer games o ☐ ☐ ☐ after dinner.

4 O ▢▢▢ one student is late for school.

5 I'm s ▢▢▢▢ hungry.

6 I want to go

swimming t ▢▢.

Practice

그림을 보고 알맞은 문장을 고르세요.

1
- (A) It is just my size.
- (B) It just is my size.
- (C) It is size just my.

2
- (A) Maybe he can come.
- (B) Can maybe he come.
- (C) He maybe can come.

3
- (A) I love too my mother.
- (B) Too I love my mother.
- (C) I love my mother too.

4
(A) I only know her by face.
(B) I know by her only face.
(C) I by face know her only.

5
(A) Maybe we can play basketball.
(B) We can play maybe basketball.
(C) We maybe play can basketball.

6
(A) It is already night.
(B) It already is night.
(C) It night already is.

Writing Activity

1 **yet**
아직

yet

2 **can**
~할 수 있다

can

3 **parents**
부모님

parents

4 **for**
~를 위해

for

5 **maybe**
아마도

maybe

6 **too**
너무

7 **only**
오직

8 **just**
딱

9 **still**
여전히

10 **now**
지금

Sam

Are you hungry?

Yes, but I can't have lunch yet.

I have to do my homework.

Lukas

Sam

I can help you.

Thank you.

Lukas

TOSEL 실전문제 ②

Situational Writing

 그림을 보고 문장을 완성하는 가장 알맞은 답을 고르세요.

1 He moves _____ .

   (A) quick

   (B) quicks

   (C) runner

   (D) quickly

2 They didn't arrive _____.

   (A) yet

   (B) just

   (C) much

   (D) already

3 A cheetah can run _____.

   (A) fast

   (B) easy

   (C) quiet

   (D) fastly

4 The turtle moves _____.

(A) bad

(B) slow

(C) badly

(D) slowly

5 He speaks _____.

(A) loud

(B) quiet

(C) loudly

(D) quietly

6 She gets up _____.

(A) very

(B) early

(C) right

(D) happy

Sentence Completion

빈칸에 들어갈 가장 알맞은 답을 고르세요.

1 The airplane can fly _____.

(A) high
(B) nice
(C) slow
(D) easy

4 He worries too _____.

(A) well
(B) very
(C) much
(D) many

2 _____ one person can go into the voting room.

(A) Only
(B) Many
(C) Much
(D) Quick

5 This pool is _____ deep.

(A) too
(B) well
(C) many
(D) better

3 _____, she misses him every night.

(A) Sad
(B) Sads
(C) Sadly
(D) Sading

6 The box is _____ heavy.

(A) too
(B) one
(C) long
(D) many

9 I _____ give him my toys.

(A) glad
(B) glads
(C) gladly
(D) gladed

7 She uses chopsticks _____.

(A) easy
(B) very
(C) easily
(D) happy

10 It is _____ to go out.

(A) so
(B) too
(C) late too
(D) too late

8 This pizza is _____ delicious!

(A) so
(B) well
(C) good
(D) great

CHAPTER 03

Unit 01

When do you go hiking?

너는 언제 등산하러 가니?

I go hiking _____.

문장과 함께 개념을 학습해보세요.

Q: When do you go hiking?　　　너는 언제 등산하러 가니?

A: I go hiking ▨▨▨▨▨.　　　나는 ▨▨▨ 등산하러 가.

전치사는 앞뒤 말이 연결되게 도와주는 역할을 해.
시간을 나타내는 말 앞에 오는 전치사는 on, in, at이 있어.

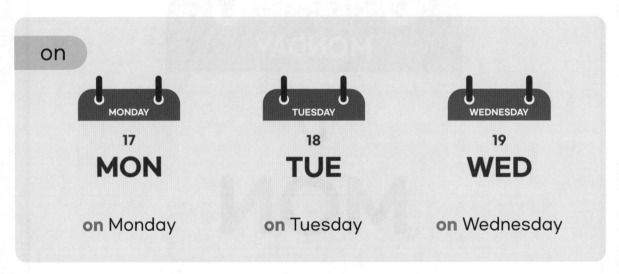

on

on Monday　　on Tuesday　　on Wednesday

in

in 2021　　in January　　in winter

at 10 o'clock   **at** noon   **at** Christmas

Activity

제시된 단어들과 어울리는 전치사를 골라 알맞은 색으로 색칠하세요.

Exercise

그림을 보고 빈칸에 알맞은 전치사를 넣어 문장을 완성하세요.

1 **We go on a picnic** _____ **Monday.**

2 **He will come** _____ **Tuesday.**

3 **Winter begins** _____ **December.**

4 You go to bed ▢▢▢ 11 o' clock.

5 The world cup is ▢▢▢ 2022.

6 I go home ▢▢▢ 6 o'clock.

Practice

그림을 보고 알맞은 문장을 고르세요.

1
(A) My birthday is at January.
(B) My birthday is in January.
(C) My birthday is on January.

2
(A) He goes to school in 8 o'clock.
(B) He goes to school at 8 o'clock.
(C) He goes to school on 8 o'clock.

3
(A) We eat lunch at noon.
(B) We eat lunch in noon.
(C) We eat lunch on noon.

4   (A) In December, there is Christmas.
     (B) At December, there is Christmas.
     (C) On December, there is Christmas.

5   (A) Our exam starts in Wednesday.
     (B) Our exam starts at Wednesday.
     (C) Our exam starts on Wednesday.

6   (A) We meet at 8 o'clock.
     (B) We meet in 8 o'clock.
     (C) We meet on 8 o'clock.

1 **on**
~에

2 **at**
~에

3 **in**
~에

4 Monday
월요일

5 Tuesday
화요일

6 Friday
금요일

Friday

7 January
1월

January

8 winter
겨울

winter

9 noon
정오

noon

10 exam
시험

exam

Unit Review

다음 대화를 완성하고, 소리내어 연습해보세요.

Minha

When do you go hiking?

I go hiking on Wednesday.

Grew

Minha

Can I join?

Of course. Let's go together.

Grew

Minha

See you on Wednesday!

Unit 02

Where are you?

너 어디에 있니?

I'm _____.

문장과 함께 개념을 학습해보세요.

Q: Where are you?   너 어디에 있니?
A: I'm   .   나는   있어.

장소랑 시간을 나타내는 전치사들은 서로 똑같이 생겼어. 장소를 나타내는 말 앞에 오는 전치사는 **on, in, at**이야.

on

on the road   **on** the corner   **on** the wall

in

in the pool   **in** the city   **in** the room

at home   at a concert   at the bus stop

Activity

다음 보기에서 그림과 어울리는 전치사를 골라 빈칸을 채우세요.

보기   at   on   in

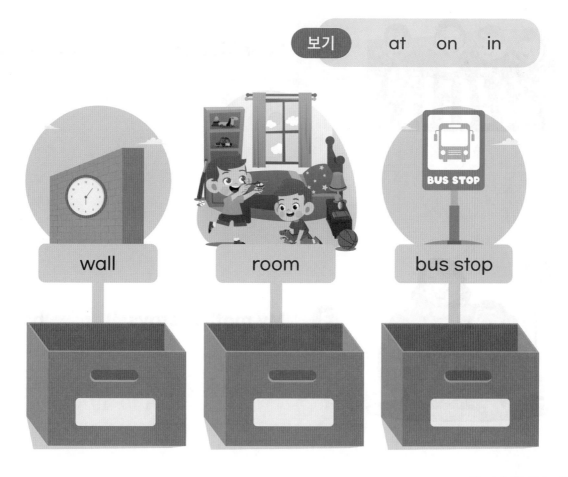

wall   room   bus stop

Exercise

그림을 보고 빈칸에 알맞은 전치사를 넣어 문장을 완성하세요.

1   **They swim** ⬚⬚⬚ **the pool.**

2   **Four kids are** ⬚⬚⬚ **the road.**

3   **My mother stays** ⬚⬚⬚ **home.**

4 There are many people _____ the bus stop.

5 I can see a lot of buildings _____ the city.

6 We watch a movie _____ the theater.

Practice

그림을 보고 알맞은 문장을 고르세요.

1
(A) The car is in the road.
(B) The car is at the road.
(C) The car is on the road.

2
(A) See the painting in the wall.
(B) See the painting at the wall.
(C) See the painting on the wall.

3
(A) She is in the hospital.
(B) She is at the hospital.
(C) She is on the hospital.

4 (A) He is in home.
(B) He is at home.
(C) He is on home.

5 (A) They are at the concert.
(B) They are in the concert.
(C) They are on the concert.

6 (A) She works an airplane on.
(B) She works on an airplane.
(C) She works an on airplane.

✏️ Writing Activity

1 hospital
병원

hospital

2 corner
모퉁이

corner

3 pool
수영장

pool

4 room
방

room

5 concert
연주회

concert

6 **road**
도로

7 **wall**
벽

8 **city**
도시

9 **home**
집

10 **airport**
공항

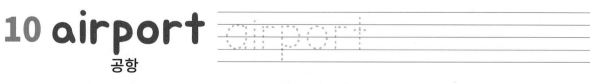

Unit Review

다음 대화를 완성하고, 소리내어 연습해보세요.

Emma

> Where are you?

> I'm at home.

Mateo

Emma

> Let's meet at the bus stop.

> Okay. Let's meet at 5 o' clock.

Mateo

Unit 03

Where is the cat?

고양이가 어디에 있니?

It is _____ the box.

문장과 함께 개념을 학습해보세요.

Q: Where is the cat?　　　　　　　고양이가 어디에 있니?

A: It is ▮▮▮▮▮ the box.　　　그것은 상자 ▮▮ 있어.

위치를 나타내는 전치사들은 다양해.
under, behind, 그리고 between처럼 긴 전치사들도 있어.

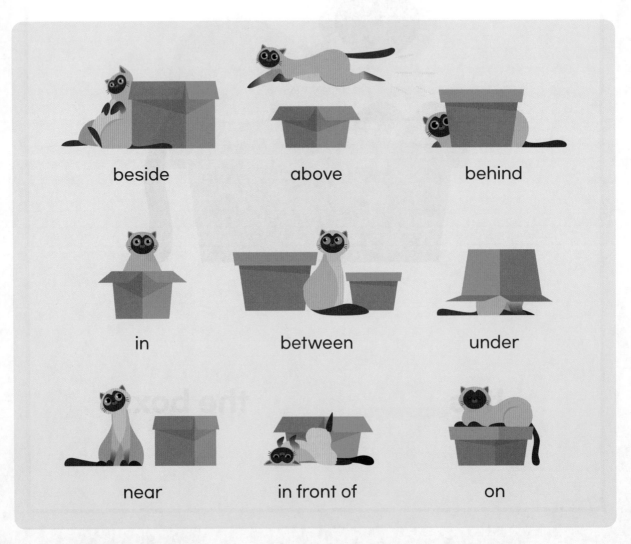

beside　　　　　　above　　　　　　behind

in　　　　　　between　　　　　　under

near　　　　　in front of　　　　　on

behind the book

under the sofa

Activity

알맞은 전치사와 연결하세요.

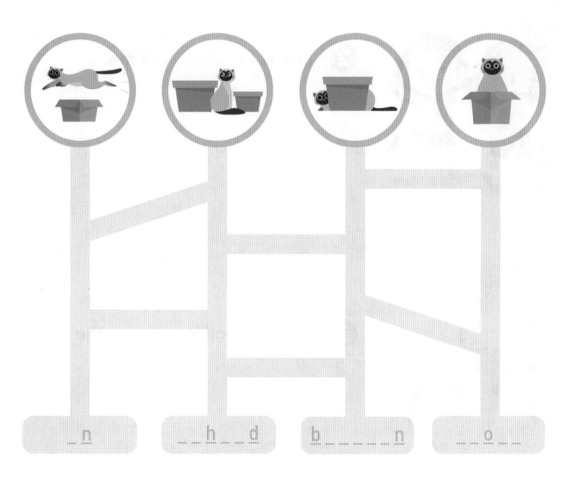

_ n

_ _ h _ d

b _ _ _ _ n

_ _ o _

Exercise

그림을 보고 빈칸에 알맞은 전치사를 넣어 문장을 완성하세요.

1 It is _____ the table.

2 He is in _____ of me.

3 Your pencil is _____ the chair.

4 Apples are ⬚⬚⬚ the basket.

5 She sits ⬚⬚⬚ the sofa.

6 He sits in ⬚⬚⬚ of the computer.

Practice

그림을 보고 알맞은 문장을 고르세요.

1. (A) The building is in the sea.
   (B) The building is on the sea.
   (C) The building is beside the sea.

2. (A) The sharks are on the sea.
   (B) The sharks are near the sea.
   (C) The sharks are under the sea.

3. (A) The dog sleeps on the sofa.
   (B) The dog sleeps behind the sofa.
   (C) The dog sleeps in front of the sofa.

4 (A) His house is above the trees.
(B) His house is between the trees.
(C) His house is in front of the trees.

5 (A) A bus stop is in the bank.
(B) A bus stop is near the bank.
(C) A bus stop is between the bank.

6 (A) A monkey is on the tree.
(B) A monkey is under the tree.
(C) A monkey is in front of the tree.

✏️ Writing Activity

1 beside
옆에

beside

2 behind
뒤에

behind

3 under
아래에

under

4 above
위에

above

5 between
사이에

between

6 near
근처에

near

7 desk
책상

desk

8 bus stop
버스 정류장

bus stop

9 basket
바구니

basket

10 sofa
소파

sofa

Unit Review

다음 대화를 완성하고, 소리내어 연습해보세요.

Liam

Where is my bag?

It is on the bed.

Charlotte

Liam

I can't find it.

Oh, I'm sorry.

It is under the desk.

Charlotte

Unit 04

What are you doing?

너는 무엇을 하는 중이니?

I am coming _____ the room.

문장과 함께 개념을 학습해보세요.

> Q: What are you doing?   너는 무엇을 하는 중이니?
> A: I am going ___ the room.   나는 방 ___ 들어가고 있어.

전치사는 방향을 나타낼 수도 있어.
위치는 멈춰있을 때, 방향은 움직일 때 사용해.

up   down   over

into   out of   through

away from   to   across

in이랑 **into**는 비슷하게 생겼지만 다른 의미야. 헷갈리는 문제니까 주의하자!

in the house

into the house

Activity

빈칸을 채워 단어를 완성하세요.

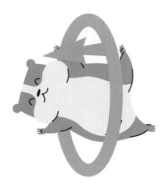

⬜ h ⬜ ⬜ g ⬜

⬜ ⬜ r ⬜ s

Exercise

그림을 보고 빈칸에 알맞은 전치사를 넣어 문장을 완성하세요.

1 He climbs _____ a mountain.

2 They walk _____ the crosswalk.

3 She goes _____ the gate.

4 He comes _____ the slide.

5 They go _____ the museum.

6 He comes _____ the room.

Practice

그림을 보고 알맞은 문장을 고르세요.

1
(A) People go into the stadium.
(B) People go out of the stadium.
(C) People go through the stadium.

2
(A) He walks to the hospital.
(B) He walks on the hospital.
(C) He walks over the hospital.

3
(A) She runs into the monster.
(B) She runs across the monster.
(C) She runs away from the monster.

4

(A) He climbs over the wall.

(B) He climbs down the wall.

(C) He climbs out of the wall.

5

(A) The ship goes to the sea.

(B) The ship goes into the sea.

(C) The ship goes across the sea.

6

(A) He passes over the window.

(B) He passes through the window.

(C) He passes away from the window.

1 **up**
위로

2 **down**
아래로

3 **over**
~위로

4 **through**
~을 통해

5 **across**
건너서

6 out of
~의 밖으로

7 into
안으로

8 away from
~에서 떠나서

9 to
~로

10 house
집

Unit Review

다음 대화를 완성하고, 소리내어 연습해보세요.

Mia

Where are you going, David?

I am going into my room.

Where are you?

David

Mia

I am in my room.

TOSEL 실전문제 ❸

Situational Writing

 그림을 보고 문장을 완성하는 가장 알맞은 답을 고르세요.

1 The boy is _____ the tree.

   (A)   in

   (B)   on

   (C)   above

   (D)   behind

2 It is _____ the box.

   (A)   in

   (B)   at

   (C)   on

   (D)   above

3 The lamp is _____ the window.

   (A)   under

   (B)   above

   (C)   beside

   (D)   behind

4 They walk _____ the classroom.

(A) in

(B) into

(C) across

(D) away from

5 The cat wants to come _____ the cage.

(A) into

(B) out of

(C) across

(D) through

6 The park is _____ my house.

(A) under

(B) behind

(C) between

(D) in front of

Sentence Completion

 빈칸에 들어갈 가장 알맞은 답을 고르세요.

1 The teacher writes down answers _____ the board.

(A) in

(B) at

(C) on

(D) near

2 The class starts _____ 9 o'clock.

(A) in

(B) at

(C) on

(D) beside

3 _____ 2022, I will be 10 years old.

(A) In

(B) At

(C) To

(D) On

4 There is a crosswalk _____ the buildings.

(A) in

(B) under

(C) above

(D) between

5 They climb _____ the mountain.

(A) to

(B) up

(C) down

(D) across

6 The car is _____ the road.

(A) in
(B) at
(C) by
(D) on

9 She jumps _____ the pool first.

(A) up
(B) into
(C) above
(D) out to

7 The holiday is _____ Thursday.

(A) in
(B) at
(C) by
(D) on

10 There is fog _____ the city.

(A) in
(B) front
(C) under
(D) between

8 Put it _____ the table.

(A) in
(B) on
(C) into
(D) between

엄선된 **100만 명**의 응시자 성적 데이터를 활용한 **AI기반** 데이터 공유 및 가치 고도화 **플랫폼**

TOSEL® Lab

공동기획
- 고려대학교 문과대학 언어정보연구소
- 국제토셀위원회

TOSEL Lab 이란?

국내외 15,000여 개 학교·학원 단체응시인원 중 엄선한 100만 명 이상의 실제
TOSEL 성적 데이터와, 정부(과학기술정보통신부)의 AI 바우처 지원 사업
수행기관 선정으로 개발된 맞춤식 AI 빅데이터 기반 영어성장 플랫폼입니다.

TOSEL Lab
지정교육기관 혜택

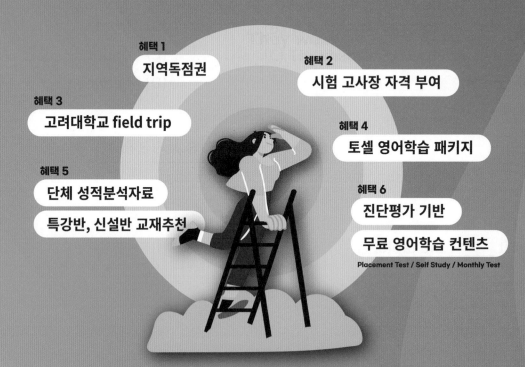

혜택 1
지역독점권

혜택 2
시험 고사장 자격 부여

혜택 3
고려대학교 field trip

혜택 4
토셀 영어학습 패키지

혜택 5
단체 성적분석자료

특강반, 신설반 교재추천

혜택 6
진단평가 기반

무료 영어학습 컨텐츠

Placement Test / Self Study / Monthly Test

학원장의 실질적인 비용부담 없이
TOSEL® Lab

브랜드를 사용할 수 있는 기회

TOSEL Lab 에는 어떤 콘텐츠가 있나요?

진단 맞춤형 레벨테스트로
정확한 평가 제공

응시자 빅데이터 분석에 기반한
테스트로 신규 상담 학생의
영어능력을 정확하게 진단하고
효과적인 영어 교육을 실시하기
위한 객관적인 가이드라인을
제공합니다.

교재 세분화된 레벨로
실력에 맞는 학습 제공

TOSEL의 세분화된 교재 레벨은
각 연령에 맞는 어휘와 읽기
지능 및 교과 과정과의 연계가
가능하도록 설계된 교재들로
효과적인 학습 커리큘럼을
제공합니다.

학습 다양한 교재연계 콘텐츠로
효과적인 자기주도학습

TOSEL 시험을 대비한 다양한
콘텐츠를 제공해 영어 학습에
시너지 효과를 기대할 수
있으며, 학생들의 자기주도
학습 습관을 더 탄탄하게
키울 수 있습니다.

Reading Series
내신과 토셀 고득점을 한꺼번에

Pre-Starter Starter Basic Junior High-Junior

- 각 단원 학습 도입부에 주제와 관련된 이미지를 통한 말하기 연습
- 각 Unit 별 4-6개의 목표 단어 제시, 그림 또는 영문으로 단어 뜻을 제공하여 독해 학습 전 단어 숙지
- 독해&실용문 연습을 위한 지문과 Comprehension 문항을 10개씩 수록하여 이해도 확인 및 진단
- 숙지한 독해 지문을 원어민 음성으로 들으며 듣기 학습 , 듣기 전, 듣기 중, 듣기 후 학습 커리큘럼 마련

Listening Series
한국 학생들에게 최적화된 듣기 실력 완성!

Pre-Starter Starter Basic Junior High-Junior

- 초등 / 중등 교과과정 연계 말하기&듣기 학습과 세분화된 레벨
- TOSEL 기출 문장과 실생활에 자주 활용되는 문장 패턴을 통해 듣기 및 말하기 학습
- 실제 TOSEL 지문의 예문을 활용한 실용적 학습 제공
- 실전 감각 향상과 점검을 위한 기출 문제 수록

Speaking Series
출간예정

Grammar Series

체계적인 단계별 **문법 지침서**

Pre-Starter | Starter | Basic | Junior | High-Junior

- 초등 / 중등 교과과정 연계 문법 학습과 세분화된 레벨
- TOSEL 기출 문제 연습과 최신 수능 출제 문법을 포함하여 수능 / 내신 대비 가능
- 이해하기 쉬운 그림, 깔끔하게 정리된 표와 설명, 다양한 문제를 통해 문법 학습
- 실전 감각 향상과 점검을 위한 기출 문제 수록

Voca Series

학년별 꼭 알아야하는 **단어 수록!**

Pre-Starter | Starter | Basic | Junior | High-Junior

- 각 단어 학습 도입부에 주제와 관련된 이미지를 통한 말하기 연습
- TOSEL 시험을 기준으로 빈출 지표를 활용한 예문과 문제 구성
- 실제 TOSEL 지문의 예문을 활용한 실용적 학습 제공
- 실전 감각 향상과 점검을 위한 실전 문제 수록

Story Series

읽는 재미에 실력까지 **동시에!**

Pre-Starter | Starter | Basic | Junior

- 초등 / 중등 교과과정 연계 영어 학습과 세분화된 레벨
- 이야기 지문과 단어를 함께 연결지어 학생들의 독해 능력을 평가
- 이해하기 쉬운 그림, 깔끔하게 정리된 표와 설명, 다양한 문제, 재미있는 스토리를 통한 독해 학습
- 다양한 단계의 문항을 풀어보고 학생들의 읽기, 듣기, 쓰기, 말하기 실력을 집중적으로 향상

교재를 100% 활용하는 TOSEL Lab 지정교육기관의 노하우!

Teaching Materials

TOSEL에서 제공하는 수업 자료로
교재 학습을 더욱 효과적으로 진행!

Study Content

철저한 자기주도학습 콘텐츠로
교재 수업 후 효과적인 복습!

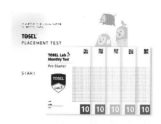

Test Content

교재 학습과 더불어 학생 맞춤형
시험으로 실력 점검 및 향상

100만 명으로 엄선된 **TOSEL**
성적 데이터로 탄생!

TOSEL Lab 지정교육기관을 위한 콘텐츠로
더욱 효과적인 수업을 경험하세요.

국제토셀위원회는 TOSEL Lab 지정교육기관에서 교재로
수업하는 학원을 위해 교재를 잘 활용할 수 있는 다양한
콘텐츠를 제공 및 지원합니다.

TOSEL Lab 지정교육기관은

국제토셀위원회 직속 TOSEL연구소에서 20년 동안 보유해온
전국 15,000여 개 교육기관 토셀 응시자들의 영어성적 분석데이터를
공유받아, 통계를 기반으로 한 전문적이고 과학적인 커리큘럼을 설계하고,
영어학습 방향을 제시하여,경쟁력있는 기관, 잘 가르치는 기관으로
해당 지역에서 입지를 다지게 됩니다.

**TOSEL Lab 지정교육기관으로 선정되기 위해서는
소정의 심사 절차가 수반됩니다.**

TOSEL Lab
심사신청

TOSEL Lab
더 알아보기

TOSEL® Lab

Answers

Short Answers

UNIT 1 Activity p.21	01. am					
	01. am / 는					
	01. (1) → is	(2) → are	(3) → are	(4) → am	(5) → is	(6) → is
Exercise p.24	01. is	02. are	03. is	04. am	05. is	06. is
Practice p.26	01. (C) They are vets.	02. (A) It is for baseball.	03. (A) She is sick.	04. (A) It is a pear.	05. (A) He is in the bank.	06. (B) I am angry.
UNIT 2 Activity p.31	01. the beach					
	01. the mountain / 산					
	01. (1) → 무엇을	(2) → 어디서	(3) → 왜	(4) → 어떻게	(5) → 누가	(6) → 언제
Exercise p.34	01. When	02. Where	03. What	04. Why	05. Who	06. How
Practice p.36	01. (C) Where is the bank?	02. (B) How are you?	03. (C) When are you going to sleep?	04. (A) Who is your teacher?	05. (C) When are they going to study?	06. (C) Where is the bakery?
UNIT 3 Activity p.41	01. likes					
	01. likes / 좋아해					
	01. (1) → 자라다	(2) → 주다	(3) → 좋아하다	(4) → 먹다	(5) → 싫어하다	
Exercise p.44	01. r / i / n / k / s	02. i / n / g / s	03. i / v / e / s	04. a / t / s	05. a / t / e / s	06. r / o / w / s
Practice p.46	01. (B) She sits on the chair.	02. (C) He closes the window.	03. (A) The birds fly in the air.	04. (A) He stands on the stage.	05. (B) She claps her hands.	06. (C) The ice melts.
UNIT 4 Activity p.51	01. swimming					
	01. playing the violin / 바이올린 연주 중이야.					
	01. O → 1, 3, 5, 6 X → 2, 4					
Exercise p.54	01. rides	02. write	03. swim	04. studying	05. dancing	06. walking
Practice p.56	01. (B) He jumps into the water.	02. (A) I use a computer.	03. (A) She runs.	04. (B) He finishes his homework.	05. (B) She washes her hands.	06. (A) They find him.
TOSEL 실전문제 1	01. (A) Why	02. (B) waits	03. (B) sell	04. (D) Where	05. (A) play	06. (B) shows
	01. (C) washes	02. (A) is	03. (C) flies	04. (A) run	05. (A) Who	06. (A) is
	07. (C) are	08. (A) is	09. (C) When	10. (C) studies		

UNIT 1 Activity p.67	01. carefully					
	01. noisily / 시끄럽게					
	01. (공부한 부사들로 빙고판을 완성하세요.) quickly, slowly, loudly, easily, quietly, badly, sadly, happily, noisily					
Exercise p.70	01. slowly	02. loudly	03. sadly	04. easily	05. quietly	06. quickly
Practice p.72	01. (B) We sing a song happily.	02. (C) He acts badly.	03. (C) She moves quickly.	04. (B) He picks a book carefully.	05. (B) The teacher treats us kindly.	04. (B) He paints nicely.
UNIT 2 Activity p.77	01. inside					
	01. outside / 밖에					
	01. (1) → 잘	(2) → 열심히	(3) → 매우	(4) → 아주	(5) → 빠르게	(6) → 오늘
Exercise p.80	01. a / r / d	02. e / r / y	03. a / s / t	04. o	05. u / c / h	06. o / d / a / y
Practice p.82	01. (B) He dances very well.	02. (A) She works hard.	03. (C) The man looks very handsome.	04. (C) We will play soccer today.	05. (C) Thank you very much.	06. (B) He swims very well.

UNIT 3	🖊	01. fast					
▶ Activity	🖊	01. fast / 빠르게					
p.87	🖊	01. (1) meet early	(2) live long		(3) think right		
▶ Exercise p.90	🖊	01. a / t / e	02. a / s / t	03. a / r / l / y	04. i / g / h / t		
▶ Practice p.92	🖊	01. (B) A monkey has a long tail.	02. (B) A horse runs fast.	03. (C) He writes the right answer.	04. (B) He lives a hard life.	05. (C) He tries hard to win.	06. (B) A monkey can climb high.
UNIT 4	🖊	01. yet					
▶ Activity	🖊	01. now / 지금					
p.97	🖊	01. (1) Maybe she is sad.	(2) I already had lunch.	(3) I love you too.	(4) She still hates you.	(5) I didn't have lunch yet.	
▶ Exercise p.100	🖊	01. o / o	02. e / t	03. n / l / y	04. n / l / y	05. t / i / l / l	06. o / o
▶ Practice p.102	🖊	01. (A) It is just my size.	02. (A) Maybe he can come.	03. (C) I love my mother too.	04. (A) I only know her by face.	05. (A) Maybe we can play basketball.	06. (A) It is already night.
TOSEL 실전문제 2	🖊	01. (D) quickly	02. (A) yet	03. (A) fast	04. (D) slowly	05. (C) loudly	06. (B) early
	🖊	01. (A) high	02. (A) Only	03. (C) Sadly	04. (C) much	05. (A) too	06. (A) too
		07. (C) easily	08. (A) so	09. (C) gladly	10. (D) too late		

CHAPTER 3							p.112
UNIT 1	🖊	01. on Monday					
▶ Activity	🖊	01. on Friday / 금요일에					
p.113	🖊	01. noon → at	January → in	Friday → on	Thursday → on	6 o'clock → at	winter → in
▶ Exercise p.116	🖊	01. on	02. on	03. in	04. at	05. in	06. at
▶ Practice p.118	🖊	01. (B) My birthday is in January.	02. (B) He goes to school at 8 o'clock.	03. (A) We eat lunch at noon.	04. (A) In December, there is Christmas.	05. (C) Our exam starts on Wednesday.	06. (A) We meet at 8 o'clock.
UNIT 2	🖊	01. at the airport					
▶ Activity	🖊	01. in the hospital / 병원에					
p.123		01. wall → on		room → in		bus stop → at	
▶ Exercise p.126	🖊	01. in	02. on	03. at	04. at	05. in	06. in
▶ Practice p.128	🖊	01. (C) The car is on the road.	02. (C) See the painting on the wall.	03. (A) She is in the hospital.	04. (B) He is at home.	05. (A) They are at the concert.	06. (B) She works on an airplane.
UNIT 3	🖊	01. on					
▶ Activity	🖊	01. under / 아래에					
p.133	🖊	01. 첫 번째 그림 → above	두 번째 그림 → between	세 번째 그림 → behind	네 번째 그림 → in		
▶ Exercise p.136	🖊	01. on	02. front	03. on	04. in	05. on	06. front
▶ Practice p.138	🖊	01. (C) The building is beside the sea.	02. (C) The sharks are under the sea.	03. (C) The dog sleeps in front of the sofa.	04. (B) His house is between the trees.	05. (B) A bus stop is near the bank.	06. (A) A monkey is on the tree.
UNIT 4	🖊	01. out of					
▶ Activity	🖊	01. into / 안으로					
p.143	🖊	01. t / r / o / u / h		(2) a / c / o / s			
▶ Exercise p.146	🖊	01. up	02. across	03. through	04. down	05. into	06. out of
▶ Practice p.148	🖊	01. (B) People go out of the stadium.	02. (A) He walks to the hopital.	03. (C) She runs away from the monster.	04. (A) He climbs over the wall.	05. (C) The ships goes across the sea.	06. (B) He passes through the window.
TOSEL 실전문제 3	🖊	01. (D) behind	02. (A) in	03. (C) beside	04. (B) into	05. (B) out of	06. (D) in front of
	🖊	01. (C) on	02. (B) at	03. (A) In	04. (D) between	05. (B) up	06. (D) on
		07. (D) on	08. (B) on	09. (B) into	10. (A) in		